ZOMBIE ANIMALS
PARASITES TAKE CONTROL!

ZOMBIE SNAILS

BY JOLENE ALESSI

Gareth Stevens
PUBLISHING

Please visit our website, www.garethstevens.com. For a free color catalog of all our high-quality books, call toll free 1-800-542-2595 or fax 1-877-542-2596.

Cataloging-in-Publication Data

Alessi, Jolene.
Zombie snails / by Jolene Alessi.
p. cm. — (Zombie animals: parasites take control!)
Includes index.
ISBN 978-1-4824-2848-3 (pbk.)
ISBN 978-1-4824-2849-0 (6 pack)
ISBN 978-1-4824-2850-6 (library binding)
1. Snails — Juvenile literature. 2. Parasites — Juvenile literature. 3. Host-parasite relationships — Juvenile literature. I. Alessi, Jolene. II. Title.
QL430.4 A44 2016
594'.3 —d23

First Edition

Published in 2016 by
Gareth Stevens Publishing
111 East 14th Street, Suite 349
New York, NY 10003

Copyright © 2016 Gareth Stevens Publishing

Designer: Samantha DeMartin
Editor: Kristen Rajczak

Photo credits: Cover, pp. 1, 7, 21 (bottom) D. Kucharski K. Kucharska/Shutterstock.com; p. 5 Igor Sirbu/Shutterstock.com; pp. 9, 15, 21 (middle) PHOTO FUN/Shutterstock.com; p. 11 BSIP/Universal Images Group/Getty Images; p. 13 pjt56/Wikimedia Commons; p. 17 Dorit Jordan Dotan/E+/Getty Images; pp. 19, 21 (top) Stu's Images/Wikimedia Commons; p. 20 pixelman/Shutterstock.com.

CPSIA compliance information: Batch #CS15GS: For further information contact Gareth Stevens, New York, New York at 1-800-542-2595.

CONTENTS

Words in the glossary appear in **bold** type the first time they are used in the text.

THE LOWLY SNAIL

Snails can be found all over North America and in many places around the world. They're members of the animal group Mollusca, which includes animals whose bodies have no backbone but are at least partly enclosed in a shell.

Lots of animals like to eat snails, such as **reptiles** and some kinds of birds and frogs. But one kind of snail has another **organism** to watch out for—a worm called *Leucochloridium paradoxum*. This parasite takes over the snail's body and brain!

TAKE-OVER TRUTHS

A PARASITE IS AN ORGANISM THAT LIVES WITH, ON, OR IN ANOTHER ORGANISM, CALLED THE HOST. PARASITES OFTEN HARM THEIR HOST AND CAN EVEN KILL IT!

Snails are also part of a smaller animal group called gastropods. Slugs are another kind of gastropod.

FRIGHTENING FLATWORM

L. paradoxum is a flatworm, which means it has a soft, flat body with no backbone when it's an adult. About 80 percent of flatworms are parasites! But *L. paradoxum* is a special kind of parasite. It needs two different hosts in order to complete its life cycle. Not only that, it has the ability to turn one of these hosts into a zombie!

L. paradoxum's first host is a snail. It's definitive, or final, host is a bird. It's in the bird that life begins for *L. paradoxum*.

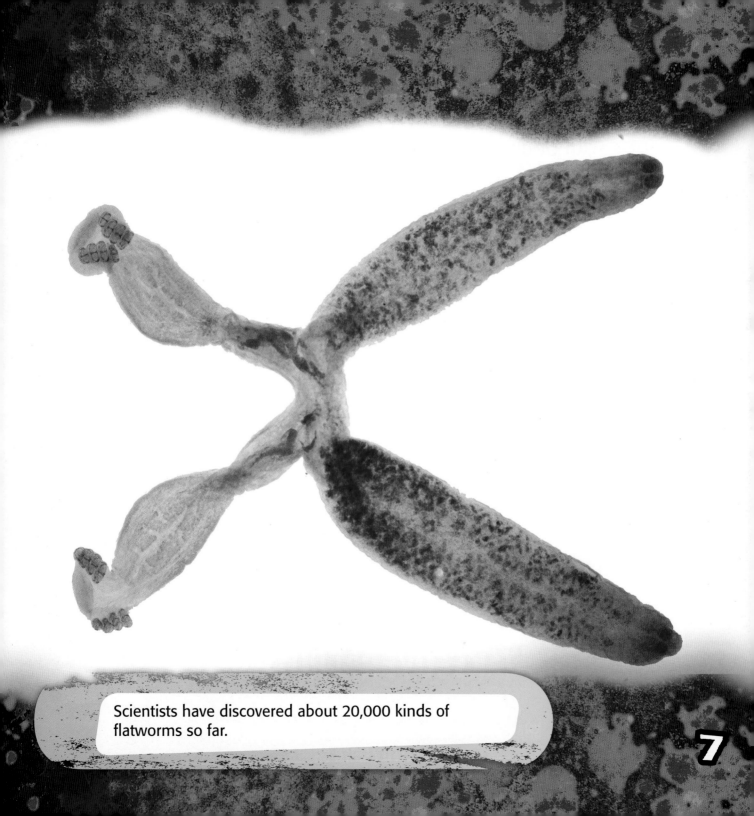

Scientists have discovered about 20,000 kinds of flatworms so far.

WORMS IN WASTE

An adult *L. paradoxum* lives in a host bird's **digestive system**. While a bird may have more than one of these parasites in its body, the number doesn't matter to *L. paradoxum*. It can **reproduce** on its own! The worm lays eggs that exit the bird in the bird's waste.

Snails eat mostly **algae** and plants, which could easily have bird waste on them. That's how a snail takes in an egg of *L. paradoxum*! Sometimes, the eggs have **hatched**, and the snail eats larvae.

TAKE-OVER TRUTHS

L. PARADOXUM ONLY WANTS TO BE EATEN BY SNAILS IN THE ANIMAL GROUP *SUCCINEA*. THESE ARE OFTEN CALLED AMBER SNAILS.

Amber snails often live in grasses and weeds.

THE SPOROCYST

Once inside the snail, *L. paradoxum's* eggs hatch if they haven't already. The larvae are covered in **cilia** that help them travel through the snail. Then, the worm larvae grow into sporocysts.

A sporocyst has three parts: a main body, a **broodsac**, and a tube connecting the two. The sporocysts look like a big mass of white inside the snail's body. They're able to grow by taking in **nutrients** from the snail through their skin.

TAKE-OVER TRUTHS

MANY *L. PARADOXUM* EGGS AND LARVAE NEVER REACH THE RIGHT HOST AND DIE.

This image shows another parasitic flatworm that **infects** snails before reaching its final host, a sheep or cow.

DISCO SNAIL

The sporocysts grow into the tentacles, or eyestalks, of the snail. The eyestalks, which are thin before a parasite infection, become swollen. They start to **pulsate** with stripes of color, including red, green, and yellow!

By this time, *L. paradoxum* has totally taken over its snail host. The snail is a zombie! Its tentacles have been made to look like big, juicy caterpillars, and the snail can't do anything about it. Scientists think the flatworm may produce chemicals to make the snail do what it wants.

TAKE-OVER TRUTHS

L. PARADOXUM IS SOMETIMES CALLED A GREEN-BANDED BROODSAC BECAUSE OF ITS COLORFUL TAKE-OVER OF SNAILS' EYESTALKS.

Since *L. paradoxum's* final host is a bird, it wants to make a snail look like a bird's favorite treat—a caterpillar!

ZOMBIE BEHAVIOR

L. paradoxum doesn't just take over a snail's eyestalks. It stops the snail from being able to reproduce. In addition, uninfected amber snails can retract, or draw in, their eyestalks. Infected amber snails with swollen eyestalks can't.

There's even stranger zombie **behavior**. Snails are nocturnal organisms, meaning they mostly come out at night. Amber snails infected with *L. paradoxum* stay out during the day. This allows birds to see them better. Somehow, the swollen eyestalks only pulsate during the day!

TAKE-OVER-TRUTHS

SCIENTISTS DON'T KNOW HOW THE PARASITIC FLATWORM KNOWS WHEN TO PULSATE. IT DOESN'T SEEM TO HAVE ANY BODY PART THAT WOULD BE ABLE TO TELL NIGHT FROM DAY.

Day can be dangerous for snails. Predators such as reptiles and mice can more easily see them—but so can the birds *L. paradoxum* wants to reach!

CATERPILLAR COPY

Birds can't tell the difference between snails infected with *L. paradoxum* and yummy caterpillars. They swoop down and grab the snail's eyestalks, infecting themselves with the parasite. When this happens, *L. paradoxum* has succeeded! It grows into an adult inside the bird and produces eggs. Then the life cycle begins again!

Sometimes, a snail's eyestalk bursts open on its own. The sporocyst will keep moving around like a caterpillar and try to draw in a bird. It often just dries out, though.

TAKE-OVER TRUTHS

ZOMBIE SNAILS ARE FOUND HIGHER OFF THE GROUND THAN UNINFECTED SNAILS, AGAIN SHOWING HOW CONTROLLED THEY ARE BY *THEIR* PARASITE!

L. paradoxum can reproduce in many kinds of birds, including crows, jays, and finches.

LIFE GOES ON

Amber snails are lucky hosts. They can live beyond a bird munching on their eyestalks! An amber snail may continue to be infected with *L. paradoxum* and controlled by it. It may grow more sporocysts and again grow the pulsating broodsac that looks like a caterpillar.

However, the snail may also be rid of the parasite. It can regrow its eyestalks and is able to reproduce again. That's good for *L. paradoxum*, too. A live snail reproducing means more live snails to infect!

Most hosts that are turned into zombies by a parasite don't live after the parasite is gone. The amber snail often does!

SNAIL STUDIES

Scientists have known about *L. paradoxum's* snail take-over since 1835! They guessed that the parasite controlled infected snails' behavior, but for a long time no one had shown it to be true. In 2013, a group of Polish scientists studied amber snails and their parasite. They proved mind control was part of the parasite-host connection!

But we don't yet know everything about *L. paradoxum* and its zombie host. As more scientists study mind-controlling parasites, there are sure to be even more cool—and creepy—facts to learn!

TAKE-OVER TRUTHS

OTHER ANIMALS BECOME ZOMBIES DUE TO PARASITES, TOO! THESE INCLUDE CARPENTER ANTS, FISH CALLED STICKLEBACKS, AND GRASSHOPPERS.

THE MAKING OF A ZOMBIE SNAIL

L. paradoxum lays eggs in a bird.

▼

Eggs leave the bird in its waste.

▼

An amber snail eats the eggs.

▼

L. paradoxum larvae grow into sporocysts in the snail.

▼

The snail's eyestalk becomes swollen, pulsates, and changes color.

▼

A bird eats the snail's eyestalk and the broodsac in it.

▼

L. paradoxum grows into an adult inside the bird.

GLOSSARY

algae: plantlike living things that are mostly found in water

behavior: the way an animal acts

broodsac: a pouch on the body of an animal where eggs or larvae grow and are held

cilia: the tiny hairlike parts of an animal body that help it move

digestive system: all the body parts concerned with eating, breaking down, and taking in food

hatch: to break open or come out of

infect: to cause to spread inside the body

nutrient: something a living thing needs to grow and stay alive

organism: a living thing

pulsate: to move at a regular rate as if to a beat

reproduce: when an animal creates another creature just like itself

reptile: an animal covered with scales or plates that breathes air, has a backbone, and lays eggs, such as a turtle, snake, lizard, or crocodile

FOR MORE INFORMATION

BOOKS

Gates, Margo. *Snails.* Minneapolis, MN: Bellwether Media, Inc., 2014.

Kopp, Megan. *Parasites.* New York, NY: AV2 by Weigl, 2012.

WEBSITES

10 Zombies of the Insect World
listverse.com/2013/03/30/10-zombies-of-the-insect-world/
Read about more zombies in nature, including ants and caterpillars.

World's Deadliest: Zombie Snails
video.nationalgeographic.com/video/worlds-deadliest/deadliest-zombie-snails
Watch a video of a zombie snail, doing exactly what the parasite wants.

INDEX

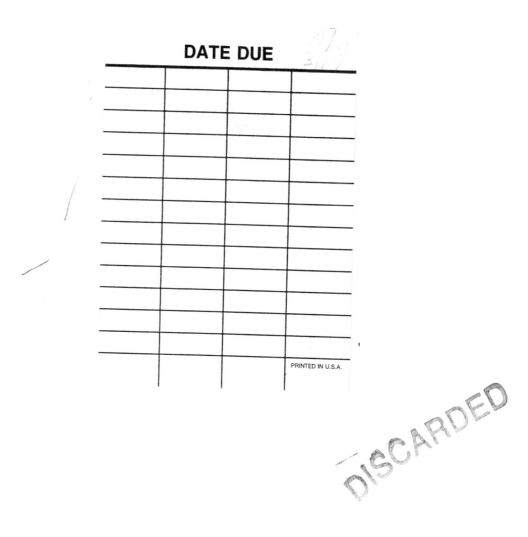

DATE DUE

PRINTED IN U.S.A.